EVERYDAY GUIDES
MADE EASY

MUSIC THEORY
COMPUTER MUSICIANS

This is a **FLAME TREE** book
First published 2015

Publisher and Creative Director: Nick Wells
Project Editor: Polly Prior
Art Director: Mike Spender
Layout Design: Jane Ashley
Digital Design and Production: Chris Herbert
Copy Editor: Anna Groves
Proofreader: Sally Brigham
Indexer: Helen Snaith
Screenshots: Rusty Cutchin
Picture Research: Gillian Whitaker

Special thanks to: Laura Bulbeck

This edition first published 2015 by
FLAME TREE PUBLISHING
Crabtree Hall, Crabtree Lane
Fulham, London SW6 6TY
United Kingdom

www.flametreepublishing.com

© 2015 Flame Tree Publishing

ISBN 978-1-78361-413-4

Printed in China

All non-screenshot pictures are courtesy of Shutterstock and © the following photographers:
1 & 126 welcomia; 3 littleny; 5 sheff; 6, 102 Pavel L Photo and Video; 8 Mikael Damkier; 10 Ischmidt; 11 aleksandr hunta; 12
photobank.ch; 13 LIUSHENGFILM; 14 DoublePHOTO studio; 19 SP-Photo; 24, 69 Daniel Fung; 27 Tatiana Popova; 28, 44 Stokkete; 34
Refat; 36, 106 Ollyy; 40 Gumenyuk Dmitriy; 46 Yellowj; 49 Umierov Nariman; 50 Kevin J King; 52 gaetano guerra; 55 Ahuli Labutin ; 57
Voyagerix; 58 Terrance Emerson; 60 TranceDrumer; 61 Andrew Lam; 62 Alzbeta; 64 Vgstockstudio; 67 David Puerto ; 71 dwphotos ; 72
Maxim Blinkov ; 77 Pressmaster; 78 Andrija Kovac; 79 Nejc Vesel ; 80 auremar; 81 Paul Keeling; 82 Andrey Armyagov; 86 Strukt; 88
Kudla ; 89 Dieter Hawlan; 90 DT10; 94 Imageman; 97 Kondor83; 98 zeljkodan; 99 Ermolaev Alexander; 104 Syda Productions; 107
Milles Studio; 108 Mikhail Rulkov; 109 Jonas Jensen; 110 Nikola Spasenoski or Goodluz; 116 S_L; 117 Ldprod; 125 Alexander Raths.

EVERYDAY GUIDES
MADE EASY

MUSIC THEORY
COMPUTER
MUSICIANS

RUSTY CUTCHIN

SERIES FOREWORD BY RONAN MACDONALD

FLAME TREE
PUBLISHING

CONTENTS

SERIES FOREWORD

While the unstoppable rise of computer technology has left no area of the creative arts untouched, perhaps the most profoundly transformed of them all is music. From performance, composition and production to marketing, distribution and playback, the Apple Mac and Windows PC – and, more recently, their increasingly capable smartphone and tablet cousins – have given anyone, no matter what their budget, the ability to create professional quality tracks in the comfort of their own home and put them online for the whole world to hear.

But while these amazing tools give you everything you need to bring your musical visions to life in exquisite detail, what's rather more difficult to come by is the knowledge required to put them to effective use – which is where this book comes in.

Music Theory for Computer Musicians is a comprehensive guide to music theory written specifically for computer musicians, taking you through all the key concepts in a succinct, easy-to-understand way. It is sure to serve as a trusty companion on your music-making journey, whether you're a total beginner or a more advanced composer/producer looking to brush up on the basics. Work through it methodically from start to finish, or keep it by your side for reference – just don't forget to give us a credit on your debut album.

Ronan Macdonald
Music technology writer and editor

INTRODUCTION

Today's amazing digital tools are just one aspect of making great music which can stand the test of time. You need some of the traditional tools as well. This book will help you understand how music truly works.

HEAR ... AND NOW

Music theory is a fancy name that covers a lot of things you already know: how notes come together to sound good. It's all basic rhythm, melody and harmony. But you can also get in much deeper if you want.

Hot Tip

Throughout the book you will find little yellow boxes – Hot Tips – giving brief handy hints and extra pieces of advice.

SMALL CHUNKS

Each chapter in this book has short paragraphs describing particular musical techniques and tips. They don't have to be read in order, just dip into individual sections as needed.

STEP-BY-STEP GUIDES

Certain examples of traditional music theory can best be explained by specific procedures. This book takes many of the processes available to you and breaks them down into easy-to-follow, step-by-step instructions.

INSIDE THE BOOK

This book is split into five chapters. The first gives an overview of basic musical concepts. The second chapter deals with notes and how they're placed in written music. Then we look at rhythm – the basic relationships that give your beats their power. Following on from that is a chapter about chords and harmony – the background support that makes your song pop out of the speakers. The final chapter provides some tips for using your computer to learn more about music theory.

MUSICAL TERMINOLOGY

In this book we use European (as opposed to American) musical terminology to describe certain elements of musical theory. The first time we use a new term we will give its American equivalent in brackets, such as bar (measure).

A NEW LANGUAGE

THE THEORY OF EVERYTHING MUSICAL

If you're a musician, a DJ or a music fan with your own studio or even just a modern computer, you may have already explored the world of beats, loops and samples. But there's another way of thinking about music that can help you make better songs and recordings.

Above: Learning music theory will give you a deeper understanding of the fundamental principles of music, which can only enhance your own compositions.

MUSIC BEYOND BITS

With a computer you can create amazing pieces of music that were impossible to make on your own just a few years ago. So why, then, would you want to learn about music theory?

WHY MUSIC THEORY MATTERS

There are several reasons why music theory can improve your modern productions and songwriting.

- Music theory can help you understand why your favourite songs and recordings have stood the test of time.

- Understanding principles like melody and harmony can help you make music that sounds new and fresh, instead of odd and off-putting.

- When you understand the logical relationships between notes, rhythm and sonic structure, you'll see possibilities you couldn't have imagined before.

The goal of this book is to expose computer musicians to the tools of traditional composing and provide a review of the principles that make for a well-balanced piece of music.

Above: Music theory can help computer musicians make better songs and productions.

COMMUNICATION – ACOUSTIC, ELECTRIC, DIGITAL

In the past, all music came from acoustic instruments. The twentieth century brought us electricity, and engineers harnessed that power to amplify the human voice and musical instruments. More recently, the digital revolution meant computers could create music as well as record and reproduce it.

Above: Until the twentieth century there was no other option to make music other than to use acoustic instruments and voice.

READING AND WRITING

When acoustic musicians began to share each other's music, the need arose for music in print. Music notation as we know it today began to be developed in Europe in the Middle Ages (although notation existed in other cultures for many thousands of years before this) and has been adapted to many kinds of music worldwide over the following centuries.

Hot Tip

Music (or musical) notation is any system used to represent aurally perceived music visually through the use of written symbols.

Reading and writing standard musical notation are essential skills for those who want to work in the fields of classical music, musical theatre or music education.

Above: Sight-reading is the reading and performing of a piece of written music the performer has not seen before.

But you don't have to be able to sight-read a piece of printed music in real time to understand music theory. After all, sheet music exists for one reason: to communicate how the music sounds!

A COMMON MUSICAL LANGUAGE

In the twentieth century untrained musicians, led by jazz and blues pioneers, began to communicate musical ideas aurally, without the need for notation. As popular music became simpler, musicians were able to talk almost exclusively in terms of chords and rhythmic techniques. Printed music was still necessary to share the full arrangement of a song but musicians could now communicate at a rehearsal just by demonstrating an idea and letting other musicians find complementary parts.

Above: Many musicians have no need for printed music, relying instead on a thorough knowledge of chords and rhythm.

DIGITAL DISCOURSE

With the computer revolution's focus on sonics and recording, a whole new lexicon was needed for musical communication. Musical arrangements used synthesizer patches, and drum parts were programmed for machines that held samples. Sampling brought not only a stunning new aural dimension to popular music but also led to the storing of entire orchestras' worth of sounds in a computer, ready to be arranged and played back by modern producers at the touch of a key.

Above: Modern computers let you work with music notation as well as simpler graphic symbols.

THE MORE THINGS CHANGE ...

Yet as much as the language of music changes, the fundamentals of musical relationships stay constant. In Western music, our ears are attuned to specific tones, and music must generally conform to those expectations. Music theory points out the constants in the relationships between notes and rhythms. Artists then find new variations, creating a wider sonic palette for listeners.

Hot Tip

Western music divides the octave into a series of 12 tones, called the chromatic scale. In that scale, the interval between adjacent tones is called a semitone or half-step.

UNDERSTANDING NOTATION

Musical notation is the way music looks on paper. Symbols and instructions indicate how music should be played and sound.

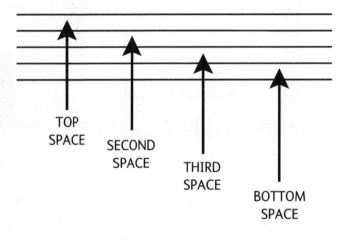

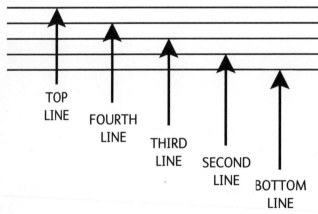

THE STAVE

In standard Western music notation, tones are represented graphically by symbols (notes) placed on a stave. The stave is a set of five horizontal lines and four spaces, each of which corresponds to a specific musical pitch or, in the case of a percussion stave, different percussion instruments. Music symbols are placed on the stave according to their pitch or function.

The lines and spaces are numbered from bottom to top; the bottom line is the first line and the top line is the fifth line.

Above: The names of the lines and spaces on the stave.

CLEFS

The pitch of each line is determined by the clef symbol on the left-hand side of the stave.

The Treble Clef

The treble clef, also known as the G clef, wraps around the second line of the stave.

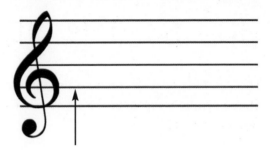

Above: The treble clef wraps around the second line.

The Bass Clef

On the bass clef (also known as the F-clef), the symbol is placed on the fourth line.

Above: The bass clef has two dots either side of the fourth line.

The Percussion Clef

For drum parts, there's the percussion clef, which assigns common instruments to spaces on the stave as shown below.

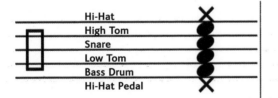

| Hi-Hat |
| High Tom |
| Snare |
| Low Tom |
| Bass Drum |
| Hi-Hat Pedal |

Above: A percussion clef with instrument note heads.

> ## Hot Tip
>
> The use of different clefs for different instruments and voices allows each part to be written comfortably on the stave.

Other Clefs

In sheet music for popular songs, the bass and treble clefs are most commonly used but other clefs, including the alto and tenor clefs, are used for other instruments in various ranges.

HITTING THE NOTES

The symbols on the stave communicate how your music should be played. These symbols represent your music, from the pitches (notes) to the silences (rests).

MIDDLE C

Which exact pitches do the treble and bass clef represent? A very important note in music is middle C. This is the C that is nearest to the middle of a keyboard. On most instruments that use the treble clef, middle C is the lowest C they can play.

Middle C is also midway between the treble and bass clefs: it is one ledger line below the treble clef and one ledger line above the bass clef. The diagrams below show where middle C can be found on the treble and bass clefs.

Hot Tip

The distance between any two musical notes is an interval. The numbers are based on scale degree rather than steps, so the interval C-D is a second, C-E is a third, and so on.

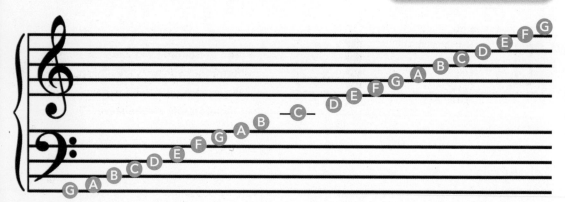

Above: A grand stave with notes of the treble and bass clefs.

Middle C is one ledger line below the treble clef

Middle C is one ledger line above the bass clef

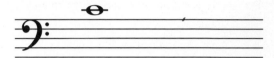

Middle C and MIDI

On MIDI keyboards, middle C is usually sounded by C4.

TREBLE CLEF NOTES

The notes of the treble clef are known as 'space notes': F, A, C, E; and 'line notes': E, G, B, D, F.
A useful way of remembering them is:

- **Space notes: F A C E**

- **Line notes: E**very **G**ood **B**oy **D**eserves **F**ootball

Playing the Notes of the Treble Clef

When the space notes and line notes are put together, they form a continuous
scale on the white notes leading up from middle C to the second A above middle C.

The diagrams below show how to find the notes of the treble clef, from middle C to A.

The notes C–A on the stave

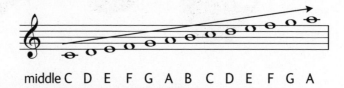

middle C   D   E   F   G   A   B   C   D   E   F   G   A

The same notes on a keyboard

middle C   D   E   F   G   A   B   C   D   E   F   G   A

BASS CLEF NOTES

The notes of the bass clef are known as 'space notes': A, C, E, G; and 'line notes': G, B, D, F, A. A useful way of remembering them is:

○ **Space notes**: **A**ll **C**ows **E**at **G**rass

○ **Line notes**: **G**ood **B**oys **D**eserve **F**ootball **A**lways

Playing the Notes of the Bass Clef

When the space notes and line notes are put together, they form a continuous scale on the white notes leading down from middle C to the second E below middle C.

The diagrams below show how to find the notes of the treble clef, from middle C to E.

The notes C–A on the stave

middle C   B   A   G   F   E   D   C   B   A   G   F   E

The same notes on a keyboard

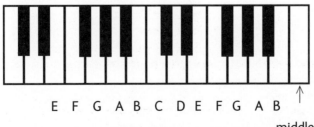

E   F   G   A   B   C   D   E   F   G   A   B

middle C

ACCIDENTALS

Note names are modified by: accidentals, sharps, flats and naturals.

Sharps

A sharp (♯) raises a note by a semitone or half-step. For example, F♯ represents F sharp.

a sharp before a note raises
that note by a semitone

Sharps are written immediately to the left of a note:

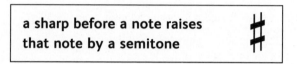

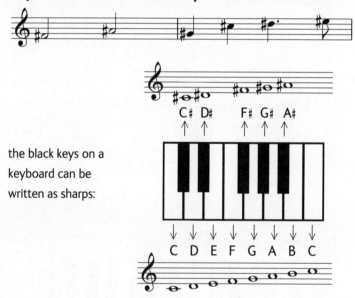

the black keys on a
keyboard can be
written as sharps:

E♯ is the same note as F and B♯ is the same note as C:

Flats

A flat (♭) lowers it by the same amount. For example, B♭ is B flat.

> **the flat symbol lowers a note by a semitone** ♭

Flats are written immediately to the left of a note:

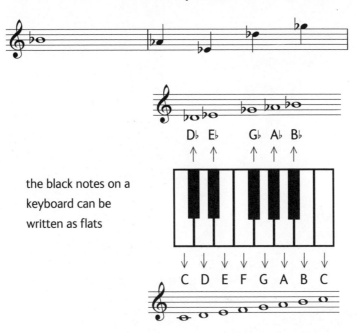

the black notes on a keyboard can be written as flats

F♭ is the same note as E and C♭ is the same note as B:

Naturals

An accidental can be cancelled within a bar by a natural (♮), which means to play the note at its original pitch, even though the key signature may have dictated that the note should be flat or sharp.

Enharmonic

If two notes have the same pitch but are represented by different letter names and accidentals, like C♯ and D♭, they are called enharmonic.

DURATION

Duration refers to a note's length (the note value). In modern popular music, the crotchet (quarter-note) is almost always the basic unit, and there are usually four of them to a bar (the smallest section of a musical piece). But music with three crotchets to the bar and other values is very common.

Note Values

Here are the most common note values (European first, followed by its American equivalent):

- **Semibreve (whole note):** Equal to eight quavers, four crotchets or two minims.

- **Minim (half-note):** Equal to four quavers or two crotchets.

Below: A semibreve lasts eight quavers, four crotchets or two minims.

- **Crotchet (quarter-note):** Equal to two quavers or half a minim.

Below: A minim lasts four quavers or two crotchets.

- **Quaver (eighth-note):** Equal to half a crotchet or two semiquavers.

Below: A crotchet lasts two quavers or half a minim.

- **Semiquaver (sixteenth-note):** Equal to half a quaver.

Below: A quaver lasts half a crotchet or two semiquavers.

Demisemiquavers (thirty-second notes) and smaller note values are common in more complex music.

Above: The relative values of the most common notes.

Dotted Notes

A note can be extended by half its length. This is indicated by a dot being placed after the note in question (see the diagram below). The most common dotted notes are:

- **Dotted minim**: Equal to six quavers or three crotchets.

- **Dotted crotchet**: Equal to three quavers.

- **Dotted quaver**: Equal to three semiquavers.

Hot Tip

If a note needs to sound beyond the border of a bar line, it is connected to a note in the next bar by a curved mark called a tie.

crotchet =
two quavers

dotted crotchet =
three quavers

minim =
two crotchets

dotted minim =
three crotchets

Above: A dot after a note means 'make the note longer by half of its value'.

STEMS, FLAGS AND BEAMS

Other than semibreves, every note placed on the stave includes a stem, and notes shorter than crotchets are indicated by flags or beams that connect them to a group of notes.

Stems

Stems are the thin, vertical lines that are directly connected to the note head. Stems may point up or down. Within one instrument voice, the stems usually point down for notes on the middle line or higher, and up for those below. If the stem points up from a note head, the stem originates from the right-hand side of the note, but if it points down, it originates from the left.

Flags

Notes shorter in length than a crotchet have flags to indicate their duration. If the stem rises from the note head, the flag will point downward from the end of the stem, and will point upward from the stem if the stem points downward.

Quavers (eighth-notes) have one flag, semiquavers (sixteenth-notes) have two flags, and so on.

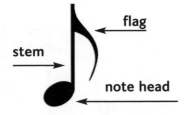

Above: Note showing note head, stem and flag.

Above: Quavers above and below middle stave line with quaver rest.

Beams

A beam is a thick line used to connect multiple consecutive quavers or notes of shorter value (indicated by two or more beams), and occasionally rests. The use of beams is called beaming.

The span of beams indicates the rhythmic grouping, usually determined by the time signature. In modern practice, beams may span across rests in order to make rhythmic groups clearer.

Notes joined by a beam usually have all the stems pointing in the same direction. The average pitch of the notes is used to determine the direction: if the average pitch is below the middle stave line, the stems and beam(s) generally go above the line; otherwise they go below.

Above: Beamed semiquavers.

RESTS

A rest is an interval of silence in a piece of music, marked by a symbol indicating the length of the pause. Each rest symbol corresponds with a particular note value. When an entire bar is devoid of notes, a semibreve rest is used. A rest may also have a dot after it, increasing its duration by half, but this is less commonly used than with notes, except occasionally in modern music notated in compound meters such as 6/8 or 12/8.

Note	Rest	British name	American name	Value
o	—	semibreve	whole note	1
♩	—	minim	half note	$\frac{1}{2}$
♩	𝄽 or 𝄽	crotchet	quarter note	$\frac{1}{4}$
♪	𝄾	quaver	eighth note	$\frac{1}{8}$
♪	𝄿	semiquaver	sixteenth note	$\frac{1}{16}$
♪	𝅀	demisemiquaver	thirty-second note	$\frac{1}{32}$
♪	𝅁	hemidemisemiquaver	sixty-fourth note	$\frac{1}{64}$

Above: Note and rest values in music notation.

KEYS AND KEY SIGNATURE

When a piece of music is centred around a certain scale, such as C major, the piece is considered to be in the key of C. This is indicated by a key signature at the beginning of the notation, immediately after the clef sign.

WHAT IS THE KEY SIGNATURE?

The number of flats or sharps next to the clef indicates the number of accidentals in the scale. A key signature tells a player which notes should be flattened or sharpened without putting a flat or sharp symbol in front of each.

Above: Key signature of A major.

CIRCLE OF FIFTHS

The circle of fifths (or circle of fourths) shows the relationships among the 12 tones of the chromatic scale, their corresponding key signatures, and the associated major and minor keys. At the top of the circle, the key of C major has no sharps or flats. Moving clockwise from the top by ascending fifths (descending fourths), the key of G has one sharp, the key of D has two sharps, and so on.

Moving anti-clockwise from the apex by descending fifths (ascending fourths), the key of F has one flat, the key of B♭ has two flats, and so on. At the bottom of the circle, the sharp and flat keys overlap, showing pairs of enharmonic key signatures.

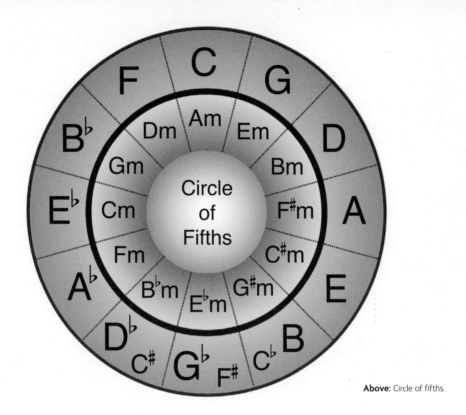

Above: Circle of fifths.

SQUARING THE CIRCLE

If you study the circle of fifths, you'll see common relationships. Every major key (like C) has a relative minor key (C's is A minor), which has the same number of sharps and flats in its key signature.

As you move from C on the circle clockwise, you add one flat to the new key's signature. Move anti-clockwise and add one sharp, and so on. Thus the key of A has three sharps in its key signature. The major scale built on F has one flat. For minor scales, rotate the letters anti-clockwise by three so that, for example, A-minor has no sharps or flats and E-minor (like its relative major key G) has one sharp.

By starting at any pitch on the circle and ascending by a fifth, you pass all 12 tones clockwise to return to the starting pitch. To pass the 12 tones anti-clockwise, you ascend by perfect fourths, rather than fifths.

Hot Tip

In music theory, distances between notes (intervals) are inclusive, so the interval from C to D (ascending) is called a second; C to E is called a third, and so on.

USING KEY SIGNATURES

In your own productions (assuming they use pitches and are not sound collages), every song will have a key, so knowing which notes work in that key will help you write better parts. That doesn't mean you have to stick with the notes of the scale. Great composers colour 'outside the lines' all the time, using notes that are outside the scale of the song's key.

Above: Key signatures.

The important thing to remember is that a key signature helps you play or write a given piece of music on paper but a key signature is not always the same as the key to the song. As we have seen, the keys of C, F and G use the same signatures as the keys of their relative minors, Am, Dm and Em respectively. But a song written in a major key has a very different sound than one written in a minor key, often described as 'happy' (major key) versus 'sad' (minor key).

DYNAMICS MARKINGS

In traditional music study, dynamics normally refers to the volume of a sound or note but can also refer to stylistic elements. These marks give the musician direction, such as when to get louder (*crescendo*) or when to play notes more smoothly (*legato*). Below is a summary of the dynamics markings you might find on printed music

piano	*p*	soft
pianissimo	*pp*	very soft
forte	*f*	loud
fortissimo	*ff*	very loud
mezzo piano	*mp*	medium soft
mezzo forte	*mf*	medium loud
crescendo	*cresc.* <	gradually louder
diminuendo	*dim.* >	gradually softer

Above: Dynamics markings.

ONWARD AND UPWARD

Now that you know something about the language of musical notation (there are many more symbols to learn if you want to read music like an expert), let's start looking at the actual notes, sounds and practical applications to help your composing and production.

EXPLORING NOTES

SCALES

In music, a scale is any set of musical notes ordered by a fundamental frequency or pitch. Scales that go up in pitch are ascending scales, while descending scales have decreasing pitch.

MAJORING IN SCALES

Understanding scales is crucial to becoming a good soloist or improviser, and knowing which scales work in what context can help with the composing process as well.

Everyone is familiar with the major scale, which corresponds to the tones, do, re, mi, fa, so, la, and ti in singing. (A final do is an octave higher than the first do.) Minor scales, modes and other scales are used in popular music

Hot Tip

The use of verbal sounds (do, re, mi, and so on) in ear-training and sight-singing is part of the method known as solfège. Studying solfège helps singers recognize musical intervals (perfect fifths, minor sixths and so on) and is a great way to better understand music theory.

TYPES OF SCALES

The major scale is the foundation of Western melody, and its seven-note set comes from the notes of the 12-tone equal temperament tuning system, which divides the octave into 12 parts. The system (known as A440) is tuned relative to a standard pitch where the A below middle C equals a frequency of 440 Hz.

CHROMATIC SCALE

Each scale step represents a semitone interval. If you play any 12 adjacent ascending notes on a piano keyboard, say from C to B, you've played a chromatic scale.

Above: The note names of the C chromatic scale, ascending and descending.

MAJOR SCALE

A major scale is defined by the interval pattern T-T-s-T-T-T-s, where T stands for whole tone (an interval spanning two semitones) and s stands for semitone. (The letters W for 'whole' and H for 'half' are often used in the US.) In an ascending C major scale, the interval between C (the tonic) and D, and between D and E, are each whole steps (whole tones) but the interval between E and F is a half-step. The rest of the intervals are whole steps, except the final one, also a half-step, from B to the C an octave above the tonic note.

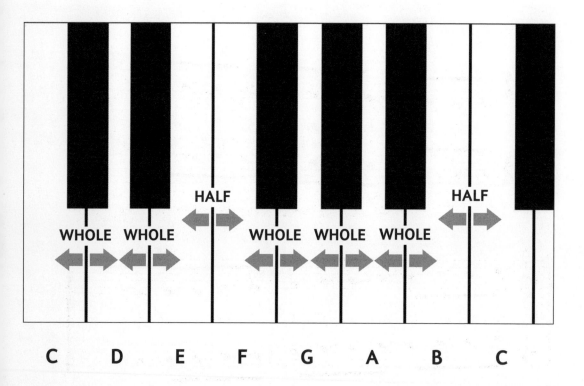

Above: The major scale always maintains the same intervals between notes.

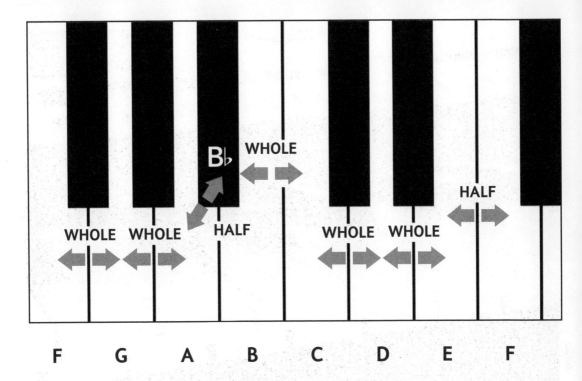

Above: An F major scale contains the same intervals as a C major scale. However, there is now a note with an accidental, B flat, at the fourth degree.

The intervals are easy to see with a C scale on a piano keyboard because there are no black keys where the half-steps occur, but the intervals stay the same no matter what major scale you play.

In notation, all seven notes of the scale must have a different letter name. This dictates whether the accidentals of a given major scale are sharps or flats. For example, in an F major scale, the fourth degree of the scale must be a semitone above the third, which is an A. That fourth note must be called B flat, not A sharp, because there is already a note with the name A in the scale.

MINOR SCALES

There are three variations on the minor scale.

Natural Minor

In its simplest form, the natural minor scale can be derived directly from the major scale with which it is most closely associated. For example, the sixth degree of the C scale is A. As we'll see when we discuss chords, the chord A-minor is the relative minor of C. The notes of the C scale played from A to A form the A natural minor scale.

Harmonic Minor

If you take those same notes and raise the seventh degree by a semitone (G to G sharp) you've created an A harmonic minor scale, which will sound very familiar to jazz fans.

Melodic Minor

You can also raise the sixth degree of the scale (F to F-sharp) and create the A melodic minor scale. However, this scale is different when it's descending. In this case the sixth and seventh degrees are flattened to their positions in the natural minor scale. These scales are used frequently in all genres of modern music.

Relative Minor: Natural

A Melodic Minor

A Harmonic Minor

Above: The three forms of a minor scale.

MODES

Modes are variations on the major scale that work with different keys to create different musical colours and textures. Essential to jazz improvisation, they can seem complicated, especially in keys with many sharps and flats, but they are essentially just the notes of one major scale beginning and ending with a note other than the scale's tonic.

Modes consist of seven scales related to the familiar major and minor keys. Although the names are Greek, they use the same set of notes as the major scale, in the same order but starting from a different note, which means a different sequence of whole and half-steps.

The interval sequence of a major scale is T-T-s-T-T-T-s, where s means a semitone and T means a whole tone. The following chart illustrates how this sequence is modified in modes.

For simplicity, the examples shown below are formed by natural notes (the white notes of a piano keyboard). However, any scale starting on any note with the same interval sequence would be a proper mode.

Mode	Tonic relative to major scale	Interval sequence	Example
Ionian	I	T-T-s-T-T-T-s	C-D-E-F-G-A-B-C
Dorian	II	T-s-T-T-T-s-T	D-E-F-G-A-B-C-D
Phrygian	III	s-T-T-T-s-T-T	E-F-G-A-B-C-D-E
Lydian	IV	T-T-T-s-T-T-s	F-G-A-B-C-D-E-F
Mixolydian	V	T-T-s-T-T-s-T	G-A-B-C-D-E-F-G
Aeolian	VI	T-s-T-T-s-T-T	A-B-C-D-E-F-G-A
Locrian	VII	s-T-T-s-T-T-T	B-C-D-E-F-G-A-B

Above: The major scale always maintains the same intervals between notes.

MODES IN REAL WORLD MUSIC

If you look at the chart on the previous page, you can quickly see some relationships.

- ○ The Ionian mode is the same as the major scale. Playing in C-Ionian mode is the same as playing a C-major scale. (All the white-key examples above relate to the key of C.)

- ○ The Aeolian mode is the same as the natural minor. Playing in A-Aeolian mode is the same as playing an A-minor scale (the natural minor form).

Dorian Mode

Dorian mode, with its semitone between the sixth and seventh degrees, creates a slight exoticism in between a natural and harmonic minor scale. Simon & Garfunkel's 'Scarborough Fair/Canticle' is a famous arrangement of a traditional melody that uses Dorian mode. The verse of The Beatles' 'Eleanor Rigby' switches between Dorian mode and natural minor.

Lydian Mode

Lydian mode puts the fourth degree of the scale on the tritone (F♯ in the key of C). The main theme from 'The Simpsons' is composed in Lydian mode.

Mixolydian Mode

In Mixolydian mode, the seventh degree is a flattened, or dominant, seventh. Legions of blues and rock soloists have used this mode for soloing. The Jacksons' 'Shake Your Body (Down to the Ground)' is a prime example of a melody in Mixolydian mode.

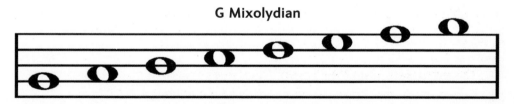

Above: Because of its flattened seventh, the mixolydian mode forms the melodies of countless blues and rock songs.

OTHER SCALES

Although there are many scales, certain ones have long been used in Western popular music. Some of the more common are:

- **The pentatonic scale (five notes):** This scale eliminates the third and seventh degrees of the major scale. The black keys on a piano (starting with C♯) form a pentatonic scale.

- **The whole tone scale**: A scale in which each note is separated from its neighbours by the interval of a whole step. The whole tone scale has a dreamlike quality, and is often used in jazz music.

- **The octatonic or diminished scale (eight notes)**: Comprising two interlocking diminished seventh chords, this scale is frequently used in jazz.

- **The blues scale**: Encompassing six-, seven- and eight-note variations, blues scales are fundamental to jazz and blues improvisation.

- **The bebop scales**: The bebop scales are frequently used in jazz improvisation and are derived from the modes of the major scale, the melodic minor scale and the harmonic minor scale.

C Whole Tone Scale

D♭ Whole Tone Scale

Above: The whole tone scale is one of the most recognizable of alternative scales.

FREQUENCY AND PITCH

It won't surprise the computer musician to learn that sound, and therefore music, is related to physics and mathematics, as is that crucial element in your music-production system – the computer. So, understanding music theory will involve some of the scientific concepts behind sound itself.

FREQUENCY

Sound is a vibration that builds as a mechanical wave. How rapidly these waves occur is called the sound's frequency.

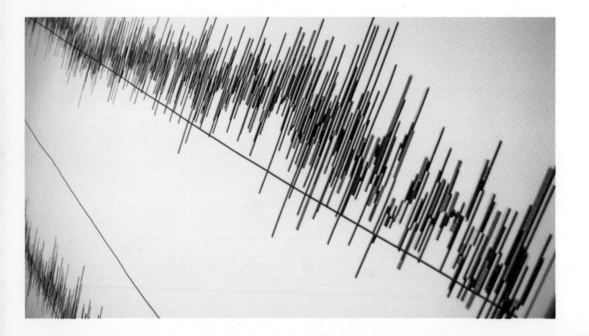

An audio frequency is a periodic vibration that is audible to the average human. It is the property of sound that most determines pitch and is measured in hertz (Hz). Audio signals have frequencies of roughly 20 to 20,000 Hz (the limits of human hearing). For more information on this, *see* the table below.

Frequency (Hz)	MIDI note	Description
8.18	C-1	Lowest organ note
16.35	C0	Lowest note for tuba, large pipe organs
32.70	C1	Lowest C on a standard 88-key piano
65.41	C2	Lowest note for cello
130.81	C3	Lowest note for viola, mandola
261.63	C4	Middle C
523.25	C5	Lowest note for a piccolo
1046.50	C6	Approximately the highest note reproducible by the average female human voice
2093	C7	Highest note for a flute
4186	C8	Highest note on a standard 88-key piano
8372	C9	
16744	C10	Approximately the tone that a typical CRT television emits while running

Above: Table of audio frequencies with corresponding MIDI note numbers and real-world sounds.

PITCH

We all know what pitch means in a musical context (someone is in tune or out of tune), but scientifically, it's a bit more complicated.

Pitch is a property of sound whose frequency of vibration is clear and stable enough to distinguish from noise. Pitch may be associated with a frequency but pitch is a subjective attribute of sound. Sound waves themselves do not have pitch. Their oscillations can be measured to obtain a frequency but it takes a human mind to perceive pitch.

Hot Tip

The total number of perceptible pitch steps in the range of human hearing is about 1,400, but the total number of notes in the equal-tempered scale, from 16 to 16,000 Hz, is just 120.

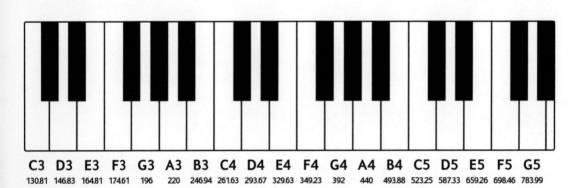

C3	D3	E3	F3	G3	A3	B3	C4	D4	E4	F4	G4	A4	B4	C5	D5	E5	F5	G5
130.81	146.83	164.81	174.61	196	220	246.94	261.63	293.67	329.63	349.23	392	440	493.88	523.25	587.33	659.26	698.46	783.99

Above: A sampling of MIDI-standard key numbers and corresponding pitch frequencies (in Hz).

PITCH STANDARDS

Concert pitch is the conventional pitch reference a group of musical instruments are tuned to for a performance. Concert pitch may vary from ensemble to ensemble, and has varied widely over musical history.

Standard pitch is a more widely accepted convention. The A above middle C is usually set at 440 Hz, although other frequencies, such as 442 Hz, are often used as variants.

Hot Tip

MIDI (Musical Instrument Digital Interface) enables modern electronic musical instruments to communicate digitally. MIDI carries event messages that include notation, pitch and velocity.

MORE ABOUT INTERVALS

You may have heard someone refer to a 'perfect fifth' or a 'diminished seventh', but how do these work exactly? Here's how they're built.

INTERVAL NAMES

The table shows the most widely used conventional names for the intervals between the notes of a chromatic scale. A perfect unison (also known as perfect prime) is an interval formed by two identical notes. Its size is zero cents. A semitone is any interval between two adjacent notes in a chromatic scale. A whole tone is an interval spanning two semitones (for example, a major second). A tritone is an interval spanning three tones or six semitones (for example, an augmented fourth).

Number of semitones	Minor, major or perfect	Short	Augmented or diminished intervals	Short	Widely used alternative names	Short
0	Perfect unison	P1	Diminished second	d2		
1	Minor second	m2	Augmented unison	A1	Semitone, half-tone, half-step	s
2	Major second	M2	Diminished third	d3	Tone, whole tone, whole step	T
3	Minor third	m3	Augmented second	A2		
4	Major third	M3	Diminished fourth	d4		
5	Perfect fourth	P4	Augmented third	A3		
6			Diminished fifth Augmented fourth	d5 A4	Tritone	TT
7	Perfect fifth	P5	Diminished sixth	d6		
8	Minor sixth	m6	Augmented fifth	A5		
9	Major sixth	M6	Diminished seventh	d7		
10	Minor seventh	m7	Augmented sixth	A6		
11	Major seventh	M7	Diminished octave	d8		
12	Perfect octave	P8	Augmented seventh	A7		

Above: The most widely used conventional names for the intervals between the notes of a chromatic scale.

INTERVAL NUMBER AND QUALITY

In Western music theory, an interval is named according to its number (also called diatonic number) and quality. For instance, major third (or M3) is an interval name in which the term major (M) describes the quality of the interval, and third (3) indicates its number.

unison   M2   M3   P4   P5   M6   M7   octave

Above: Diatonic intervals in C.

NUMBER

The number of an interval is the number of stave positions it encompasses. Both lines and spaces are counted, including the positions of both notes forming the interval. For instance, the interval C-G is a fifth (denoted P5). The table and the figure below show intervals with numbers ranging from 1 to 8. Intervals with larger numbers are called compound intervals.

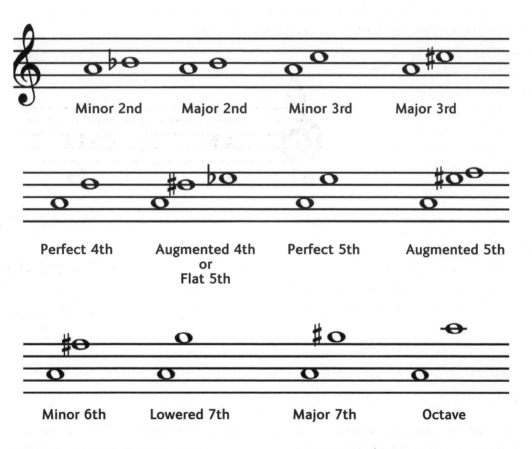

Above: Intervals from note A increasing by half-steps.

QUALITY

Intervals can also have qualities, including perfect (P), major (M), minor (m), augmented (A) and diminished (d).

Perfect

Perfect intervals are so-called because they were traditionally considered perfectly consonant: pleasant and melodious sounding. Conversely, minor, major, augmented or diminished intervals are typically considered to be less consonant, also known as dissonant: harsh or unpleasant sounding. *See below for more on consonance and dissonance.*

Major and Minor

Minor intervals occur when a major interval is made one half-step smaller. Minor intervals are labelled with a small 'm'.

Above: If the note above is in the major scale of the note below, the interval is major; otherwise, it is minor.

Within a diatonic scale, unisons and octaves are always qualified as perfect, fourths as either perfect or augmented, fifths as perfect or diminished, and all the other intervals (seconds, thirds, sixths, sevenths) as major or minor.

Augmented/Diminished

Augmented intervals are when a major or perfect interval is made one half-step larger and the interval number does not change.

Diminished intervals are created when a perfect or minor interval is made one half-step smaller and the interval number is not changed.

You may encounter any of these interval names:

- **P1**: This is perfect unison.

- **M7**: This is a major seventh.

- **m2**: This is a minor second.

- **A6**, **Aug 6**, **+6**: These are all augmented sixths.

- **d3**, **deg.5**, **dim 5**, **°5**: These are all diminished fifths.

Consonance and Dissonance

Consonant intervals are intervals that are stable. These intervals require no resolution and the sound they create together is pleasant. The consonant intervals are P1, m3, M3, P4, P5, m6, M6 and P8. All other intervals within the octave are said to be dissonant. Dissonant intervals sound tense and unpleasant when played, and require resolution to a stable (consonant) interval.

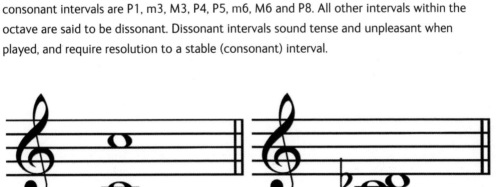

Above: The interval on the left, a perfect octave, is a consonant interval; the minor second, on the right, is a dissonant interval.

MORE ABOUT SOUND

We react more favourably to higher-pitched sounds than to lower-pitched sounds. Higher-pitched notes also convey more urgency.

TONE COLOUR

The tone colour, or character of an instrument is made up of three basic components:

- Attack
- Timbre
- Decay

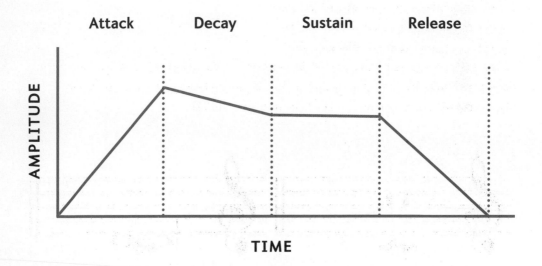

Above: Typical envelope of a generated sound. The sustain portion of the sound corresponds to timbre.

Above: Instruments such as the violin have slow attacks: it takes the full sound time to develop.

Attack

The attack is the very first sound you hear when a note sounds. When you hear the first microsecond of a snare drum, you know it's a snare because of that quick, raw sound of a stick hitting a drum skin.

The attack of a violin is completely different. The rougher texture of a bow moving across a string is just as recognizable, but is followed by a much longer sound.

Above: A snare drum has a very fast attack.

Timbre

The harmonic content of an instrument is what determines the middle part, or timbre, of a note. Surprisingly, the timbres of some very different instruments can sound very similar if you remove the attack and decay portions of the sound.

Decay

Decay is the final part of an instrument's played note. There are two types of instrument decay:

- **Impulsive**
- **Sustained**

Instruments like drums, guitars and pianos must be struck repeatedly or their sound is lost. They have an **impulsive** decay.

Instruments that can sustain for longer periods, such as violins and brass instruments, have **sustained** decays. Electronic effects like compression and distortion have given electric guitars the capabilities of sustained decay instruments.

ACOUSTICS

When you hear an orchestra or big band, you should notice two things. First, all the performers playing the same instruments are sitting together. That's because similar instruments sound louder and fuller when grouped. Secondly, the lead instruments are in front of all the other instruments, especially in acoustic performances like chamber music ensembles. This is because the sound waves from the instruments in the front of the orchestra pit will be heard a split second before the rest of the orchestra, and will thus be perceived as being louder.

Hot Tip

Vibrations cause air particles next to the source to vibrate as well, and those air particles cause the particles next to them to vibrate, creating what we call a sound wave.

HARMONICS

Any sound, no matter what the source, is caused by something vibrating. Without vibration, there can be no sound. Just like a wave in water, the further out the sound wave moves, the weaker it gets, until it completely dissipates. If the original vibration creates a strong enough wave, it eventually reaches your ears and registers as a sound.

Above: Electric guitars with heavy distortion have the characteristics of sustained decay instruments.

When we hear a sound, it's because air vibrates against our eardrums, causing them to vibrate. These vibrations are analysed by our brains and registered as music, traffic, birdsong, and so on.

RHYTHM INTO BEATS

BEATS AND RHYTHM

Whether you're an accomplished drummer with expert miking technique or a master programmer with a warehouse full of loops and patterns dating back to the original Linn Drum and MPC60, you'll benefit from knowing the rhythmic underpinnings of music. So let's start with the basics of rhythm.

TAKING THE PULSE

Every kind of popular music depends on a regular pulse that imparts a natural rhythm in the same way the human heartbeat dictates the rhythm of life. This is true whether or not there is a single percussion instrument or a set of them keeping an audible beat.

Understanding a piece of music requires identifying this pulse, and in fact different people can hear a different pulse within the same piece of music not anchored by a recognizable beat pattern.

This pulse may change in different sections of the same piece of music, slowing down or speeding up, or occurring in a totally different pattern than the one in which it started. In most cases, as we know, there will be an unmistakable audible rhythm pattern created by recognizable percussion instruments that repeat at a certain rate.

Hot Tip

The abbreviation BPM (beats per minute) is the standard measure for both the tempo of modern music and the rate of a human's heartbeat.

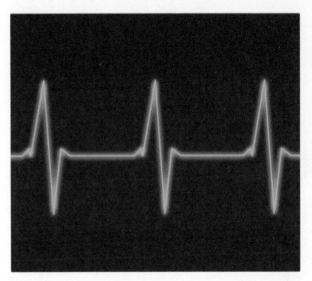

Above: Rhythm starts with the most basic beat of all: the one of the human heart.

Above: Rhythm pattern created by notes of different duration: semibreve, minim, crotchet and quaver.

TEMPO

Tempo is the speed or pace of a given piece of music. The tempo of a piece is usually indicated at the start of a piece of music in BPM. That means that a particular note value (for example, a crotchet) is specified as the beat, and the amount of time between successive beats is a specified fraction of a minute.

With modern electronics, BPM is a very precise measurement. Music sequencers use the BPM system to denote tempo. In electronic dance music, accurate knowledge of a tune's BPM is important to DJs for the purposes of beatmatching (*see* page 72).

TEMPO TALK

Some musical pieces don't use numerical beat indicators. In classical music it is customary to describe the tempo of a piece by the use of Italian words like *allegro* or *presto*.

Some of the more common tempo indicators include:

- **Grave**: Very slow (25–45 BPM).

- **Lento**: Slowly (45–50 BPM).

- **Adagio**: Slow and stately (literally 'at ease') (60–72 BPM).

- **Andante**: At a walking pace (84–90 BPM).

- **Moderato**: Moderately (96–108 BPM).

- **Allegro moderato**: Moderately fast (108–112 BPM).

- **Allegretto**: Close to but not quite *allegro* (112–120 BPM).

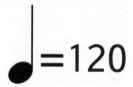

Above: Tempo markings that reference beats per minute are common in modern music.

○ *Allegro*: Fast, quickly and bright (120–28 BPM).

○ *Vivace*: Lively and fast (132–44 BPM).

○ *Presto*: Extremely fast (168–200 BPM).

○ *Prestissimo*: Even faster than *presto* (200 BPM and over).

Terms for tempo change:

○ *Ritardando*: Gradually slowing down.

○ *Accelerando*: Gradually accelerating.

Hot Tip

Most tempo indicators in classical music are Italian because tempo indications were first used extensively in the seventeenth century, when many of the most important composers were Italian.

TIME SIGNATURES AND BPMS

Like a key signature, the time signature appears at the beginning of a piece of music. It's expressed as two numbers, one above the other. The bottom number tells us what unit equals one beat (usually a crotchet) and the top number tells us how many of these beats are included in one bar.

Simple time signatures	
4 4 (quadruple)	Also known as common time: Most common time signature in rock, blues, country, funk and pop.
2 2 (duple)	*Alla breve*, or cut time: Used for marches and fast orchestral music. Frequently occurs in musical theatre.
2 4 (duple)	Used for polkas or marches.
3 4 (triple)	Used for waltzes, country ballads, R&B, sometimes used in pop.

Above: This chart shows the styles of music that simple time signatures are most frequently used in.

OTHER TIME SIGNATURES

Time signatures don't always stay consistent throughout a song, and they don't always conform to tidy divisions of two and three. There are complex time signatures such as 5/4 and 7/4. Two well-known examples of the 5/4 time signature are Dave Brubeck's 'Take 5' and Lalo Schifrin's 'Mission: Impossible Theme'. Pink Floyd's 'Money' is in 7/4.

More common, in rock music especially, are mixed meter songs in which the time signatures change for certain sections of the song. There are many examples of this in The Beatles' music, such as 'We Can Work It Out' (4/4 to 3/4), 'All You Need is Love' (7/4 to 4/4) and 'Here Comes the Sun' (4/4 to 5/4).

Hot Tip

The most common simple time signatures are 2/4, 3/4 and 4/4.

DANCE MUSIC

Although essential to written music and the musicians who depend on it in performance, in modern popular music performance time and tempo are often indicated by a verbal count-off, the speed of which and the numbers used being usually enough to let musicians know how the song should be played.

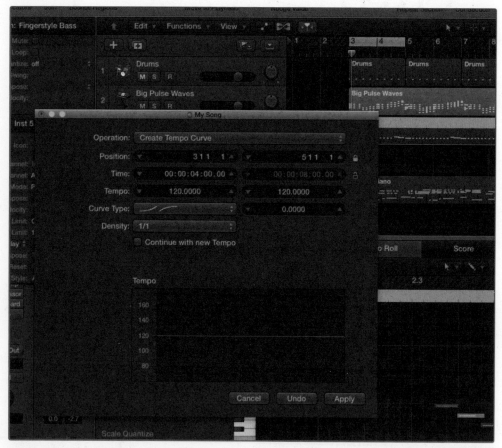

Above: Modern music software, such as Apple's Logic Pro X shown here, gives you precise and extensive control over the tempo of a song.

Beats Per Minute

When the performance depends on recordings, as with a DJ matching tempos of records in a live set, BPM became common terminology in disco because of its usefulness to DJs, and remains important in dance music.

Tempos of some dance music styles	
Typical disco	120
House	120–28
Trance	125–50
Drum and bass	150–85

Above: This chart shows the tempo of some of the most popular types of modern dance music.

The beats measured are either crotchets or other percussion beats (typically, bass drum or a similar synthesized sound), whichever is more regular.

In other genres like jazz, which is not generally composed for modern dancing, tempos may be far afield of these numbers and it's not unusual to see BPMs in the two or three hundreds.

BEATMATCHING

Beatmatching is a technique used by DJs that involves speeding up or slowing down a record in order to match the tempo of a previous track so both can be seamlessly mixed.

High and Low Tempos

DJs often beatmatch the underlying tempos of recordings, rather than their strict BPM value suggested by the kick drum, particularly when dealing with high-tempo tracks. A 240 BPM track, for example, will match the beat of a 120 BPM track without slowing down or speeding up, because both will have an underlying tempo of 120 crotchets per minute. Thus, some soul music (around 75–90 BPM) can be mixed well with a drum and bass beat (from 150–85 BPM).

Time-stretching

When speeding up or slowing down a record on a turntable, the pitch and tempo of a track are linked: spin a disc 10 per cent faster and both pitch and tempo will be 10 per cent higher. Software processing to change the pitch without changing the tempo, or vice versa, is called time-stretching or pitch-shifting. While it works fairly well for small adjustments (± 20 per cent), the result can be noisy and unmusical for larger changes.

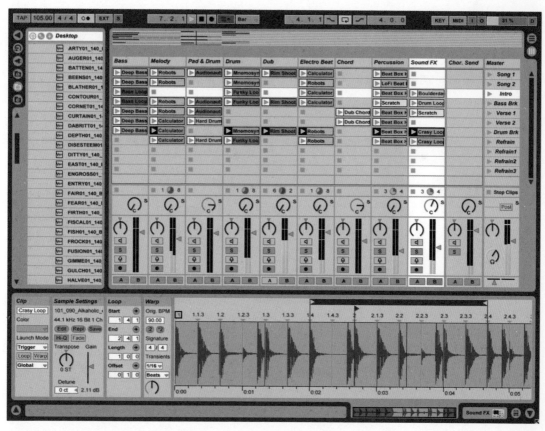

Above: Ableton Live is popular software that makes it easy to match beats from various clips.

MORE ON METER

In music and music theory, the beat is the basic unit of time, or the pulse. In popular use, beat can refer to a variety of concepts including tempo, meter, specific rhythms and groove. There are basic rhythmic devices that appear in almost all pop music.

COMMON RHYTHMIC DEVICES

In many pop songs you will run across patterns that break from the basic beat indicated by the time signature. Some of these include the following:

Above: Four basic rock drum grooves in 4/4 time.

Triplets

A triplet is a note value divided into three equal parts. Take a minim as an example. If you divide it in two, you get two crotchets. If you divide in into four, you get four quavers. There is no note value for dividing it into three, so three crotchets are written with a bracket and the number '3' written above or below them.

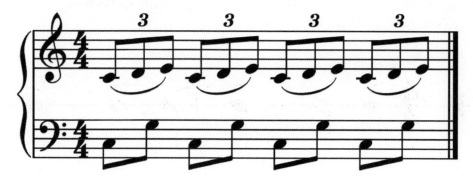

Above: Quaver triplets played against a straight quaver bass line.

The three triplets fit exactly into the next note value up: three triplet crotchets fit into a minim; three quaver triplets fit into a crotchet; and three semiquaver triplets fit into a quaver.

Triplets are often used for emphasis when one section transitions to another. They are common in songs built on mid-tempo shuffles, like Michael Jackson's 'The Way You Make Me Feel' or Whitney Houston's 'I'll Be Your Baby Tonight'. The intro to the classic rock'n'roll song 'Rockin' Robin' has fairly obvious triplets in its repeating lyrics 'Twiddily diddily de'.

Polyrhythms

Polyrhythm is the simultaneous use of two or more conflicting rhythms. Polyrhythms can be as simple as a two-beat pattern played at the same time as a three-beat pattern ('two against three') or as complex as the multiple mixed metered rhythms in modern jazz. But there are examples everywhere, from the stuttering rhythms in The Beatles' 'Happiness is a Warm Gun' to the 4:3 cross-rhythms in Britney Spears' 'Till the World Ends'.

SYNCOPATION

When you start a production, you may instinctively know the kind of beat with which you want to build your song. It may be a dance tune that requires the standard foundation – a steady crotchet kick drum ('four on the floor') at 120 BPM.

Hot Tip

When a beat gets complex, with lots of rhythmic variation, it's said to be syncopated.

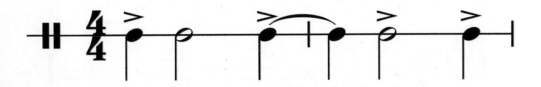

Above: A simple example of syncopation, with two points of syncopation where the third beat and first beat of the second bar are sustained from previous beats.

But if every other instrument in the mix were also restricted to crotchet downbeats, your production would get boring, and fast! Other notes and sounds need to come in between those downbeats – on the quaver 'upbeats' and other subdivisions of the beat.

GETTING IN SYNC

In music, syncopation involves a variety of rhythms that are in some ways unexpected and make part or all of a tune or piece of music feel 'off-beat'. More simply, syncopation is a general term for an interruption of the regular flow of rhythm.

All dance music makes use of syncopation and it's often a vital element that helps tie the whole track together. In the form of a backbeat, syncopation is used in virtually all contemporary popular music.

ON THE DOWNBEAT (OR NOT)

In 4/4 time, counted as 1 2 3 4, 1 2 3 4, etc., the first beat of the bar (downbeat) is usually the strongest accent in the melody and the likeliest place for a chord change. The third is the next strongest: these are 'on' beats. The second and fourth – the 'off' beats – are weaker. Subdivisions (like quavers) that fall between the pulse beats are even weaker.

You can hear the effect of 'on' and 'off' beats yourself by repeatedly counting to four and repeatedly emphasizing different beats (bold denotes a stressed beat):

- ○ *1* 2 3 4 *1* 2 3 4: The typical pattern with the emphasis on the downbeat.

- ○ *1* 2 *3* 4 *1* 2 *3* 4: The stress here is on all the 'on' beats.

But you can syncopate that pattern and alternately stress the odd and even beats, respectively:

- ○ 1 *2* 3 *4* 1 *2* 3 *4*: The stress is on the 'unexpected' or syncopated beat.

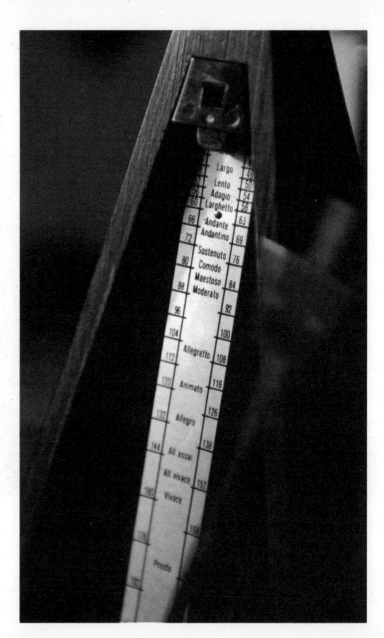

Off-beat is commonly applied to syncopation that emphasizes the weak, even beats of a bar, as opposed to the usual downbeat. This is a fundamental technique of African polyrhythm that was embraced in popular Western music. Certain genres tend to emphasize the off beat, and the technique is a defining characteristic of rock'n'roll and ska music, amongst other genres.

Above: A typical snare drum pattern of on-off beats.

BACKBEAT

A backbeat is a syncopated accentuation on the 'off' beat.

Pronounced Backbeats

R&B emerged in the 1950s largely because of pronounced backbeats that make the music highly danceable. An early record with an emphasized backbeat throughout was 'Good Rockin' Tonight' by Wynonie Harris in 1948. There is a hand-clapping backbeat on 'Roll 'em Pete' by Pete Johnson and Big Joe Turner, recorded in 1938.

Hot Tip

In a simple 4/4 rhythm, accenting beats 2 and 4 creates the backbeat.

Slap Bass

Styles of country music of the 1930s featured slap bass on the backbeat, and the late 1940s/early 1950s music of Hank Williams reflected a return to a strong backbeat as part of the honky-tonk style of country. A slapping bass style helped drive a rhythm that came to be known as rockabilly, one of the early forms of rock'n'roll.

Double Backbeat

In today's popular music the snare drum is typically used to play the backbeat pattern. Early funk music, such as James Brown's, often delayed one or more of the backbeats to further

syncopate the groove. Some songs, such as The Beatles' 'Please Please Me' and 'I Want to Hold Your Hand', employ a double backbeat pattern. In a double backbeat, one of the off beats is played as two quavers rather than one crotchet.

Above: Dance music has spawned multiple rhythms from all over the world.

EXAMPLES OF POPULAR BEATS

Here are common examples of popular dance rhythms in notation. You can see from the deviations from standard 4/4 time how syncopated the rhythms are. Understanding these in rhythm notation will enable you to program them into a DAW (*see* page 112).

Rock

Tempo: Varying
Placement: On the beat
Feel: Even

Swing

Tempo: Wide range

Placement: Varies

Feel: Triplet

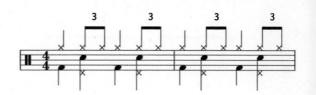

Reggae

Tempo: Slow to medium

Placement: Behind the beat

Feel: Varying degrees of swing

Hip Hop

Tempo: Slow to medium

Placement: Behind or on the beat

Feel: Varying degrees of swing

Funk

Tempo: Medium

Placement: On the beat, but can vary

Feel: Even or swing

Ska

Tempo: Medium to fast

Placement: On the beat

Feel: Even or slight swing

Disco

Tempo: Medium dance tempo
Placement: On the beat
Feel: Even

Double Bass

Tempo: Medium to fast
Placement: On the beat
Feel: Even

Ballad

Tempo: Slow
Placement: Slightly behind the beat
Time: Even or slight swing

Pop

Tempo: Medium to fast
Placement: On the beat
Feel: Even or slight swing

Punk

Tempo: Fast
Placement: On top of the beat
Feel: Even

Second Line

Tempo: Mid to fast
Placement: Behind the beat
Feel: Swing

Country Train Beat

Tempo: Medium to fast
Placement: On the beat
Time Feel: Even or swing

Latin

Tempo: Wide range depending on style
Placement: Varying
Feel: Varying

Slow Blues

Tempo: Slow
Placement: Behind or on the beat
Feel: Even

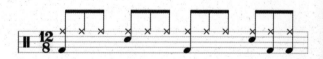

Shuffle

Tempo: Medium to fast
Placement: On the beat
Feel: Even

CHORDS AND HARMONIES

ASSEMBLING THE ELEMENTS

Now you've got the recipe and basic ingredients – an understanding of the notes and rhythms of Western music – let's get to the spices and flavourings that make this a meal, starting with the hearty stock at the foundation of the feast.

HARMONY

In music, harmony is the use of simultaneous pitches (tones, notes) or chords. The study of harmony involves chords, their construction and progressions, and the principles of connection that govern them.

In popular and jazz harmony, chords are named by their root, with various terms and characters indicating their qualities. In many types of music, including modern and jazz, chords are often augmented with 'tensions'. A tension is an additional chord member that creates a relatively dissonant interval in relation to the bass. Typically, a dissonant chord (chord with tension) 'resolves' to a consonant chord.

Harmonization usually sounds pleasant to the ear when there is a balance between the dissonant and consonant sounds – the 'tense' and 'relaxed' moments.

CHORDS

A chord, in music, is any harmonic set of two or more notes that is heard as if sounding simultaneously. The most frequently encountered chords are triads, so called because they consist of three distinct notes. Further notes may be added to give seventh chords, extended chords or added tone chords.

Above: A C major triad.

A series of chords is called a chord progression. Chords are numbered, using Roman numerals, upwards from the keynote (for more on this, *see* page 92).

Chord Charts

Common ways of notating or representing chords in Western music other than conventional staff notation include Roman numerals and various systems of chord charts typically found in the lead sheets used in popular music. As pop music has become more improvisational in nature, rough chord charts may be all that is needed for a musician to play accompaniment chords or improvise a solo.

TRIADS

A triad is the simplest type of chord and consists of three notes. Written on a stave, the triad has a distinctive look, as the three notes are written either on successive spaces or on successive lines. A triad consists of:

- **The root**

- **The third**: This a major third (four semitones) or a minor third (three semitones) above the root.

- **The fifth**: This is a note another major or minor third above the previous note. From the root, this note can be a diminished fifth (six semitones), perfect fifth (seven semitones), or augmented fifth (eight semitones).

Above: C Triads.

CHORD BUILDING

Chords are the foundational groups of notes that create harmonies and form accompaniment to singers in almost every kind of popular music. They can be very simple or extremely complex. In order to write your own music, it's important to understand how these essential building blocks work.

Using Roman Numerals

Fundamentally, chords are built on notes in the major scale. These chords are assigned Roman numerals, so that you can understand the relationships in any key. For example, in the key of C, the C major chord (Roman numeral I) is a triad built with the notes C, E, and G. Each note pair (C to E and E to G) forms an interval of a third.

Chord Progressions

If we build triads with the same intervals on every degree of the ascending C scale, we get the chords C-Dm-Em-F-G-Am-Bdim or I-ii-iii-IV-V-vi-vii. We use lower-case Roman numerals to indicate minor and diminished chords, so in any key, the most basic chords can be indicated as

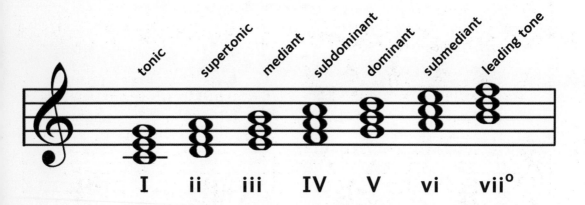

Above: Key of C chords with Roman numerals and diatonic function.

Triads							
Major	I	ii	iii	IV	V	vi	viio
Minor	i	iio	III	iv	V	VI	viio

Seventh chords							
Major	IM7	ii7	iii7	IVM7	V7	vi7	Viiø7
Minor	i7	Iiø7	IIIM7	iv	V7	VIM7	Viio7
Key: M7 = major 7; o = diminished; o7 = diminished 7; ø7 = half-diminished 7							

shown in the chart above. As chords become more complex, such as adding a 7th to the tonic chord (C-E-G-B), the same rules apply.

In practice, popular chord progressions are often referred to by their numeric equivalents, such as ii-V-I (Dm-G-C in the key of C) or I-vi-ii-V (C-Am-Dm-G).

Have A Go!

Voicing these chords on a piano keyboard is the way to familiarize yourself with their sound. You will notice recognizable tonalities that come from the worlds of pop and jazz. For example, in the key of C, the first degree (I^{M7}) in the scale of seventh chords is spelled C-E-G-B. This is the same chord at the third degree in the key of C's relative minor A.

COMMON CHORD PROGRESSIONS

A chord progression (or harmonic progression) is a series of musical chords that establishes a tonality founded on a key, root or tonic chord and that is based upon a succession of root relationships. Here are some common chord progressions in popular music.

THE 12-BAR BLUES

Probably the most foundational progression in rock'n'roll, it goes back to the nineteenth century and evolved through rural blues groups to small jazz ensembles to the boogie-woogie piano style to the earliest rock records like Jackie Brenston's 'Rocket 88' and Bill Haley's 'Rock Around the Clock'. It's the basis for Chuck Berry's 'Johnny B. Goode', Leiber and Stoller's 'Kansas City' and Robert Johnson's original and Eric Clapton's (with Cream) version of 'Crossroads' (or 'Crossroad Blues').

The Basic Chords

The form breaks down to three groups of four bars – a C-major chord (the tonic chord) for four bars, an F-major chord (the subdominant chord) for two bars, then a return to C for two bars. Finally, in the third group, there's a G-major (the dominant) for two bars and a C for two bars before repeating the entire 12 bars.

12-bar blues Roman-numeral notation			
I	I	I	I
IV	IV	I	I
V	V	I	I

Above: The 12-bar blues progression is one of the most common in jazz and rock.

There are many variations on this sequence. You can change the colour of the basic chords (C, F and G) by adding a dominant seventh note to each (Bb, Eb and F respectively). You can substitute other chords at the intersections without fundamentally changing the 12-bar blues character.

12-bar blues quick-change variation			
I	IV	I	I
IV	IV	I	I
V	IV	I	I

Above: The quick-change variation uses the subdominant chord in the second bar.

Above: The 50s progression has been in hundreds of popular songs.

THE 50S PROGRESSION

The 50s progression is a chord progression and turnaround used in Western popular music. As the name implies, it was common in the 1950s and early 1960s and is particularly associated with doo-wop. It has also been called the 'Stand by Me' change, and the doo-wop progression.

The progression, represented in Roman numerals, is I-vi-IV-V. So, for example, in C-major it would be C-Am-F-G.

THE II-V-I PROGRESSION

The ii-V-I progression is a common cadential chord progression used in a wide variety of musical genres. It is a succession of chords whose roots descend in fifths from the second degree (supertonic) to the fifth degree (dominant) and finally to the tonic.

The ii-V-I has been used for a hundred years and is found in virtually every type of popular music, including jazz, R&B, pop, rock and country. Early examples include 'Honeysuckle Rose' (1929) by Fats Waller, which features several bars in which the harmony goes back and forth between the II and V chords before finally resolving on the I chord, and Duke Ellington's 'Satin

Doll' (1953). More modern examples include the bridge of 'Everybody's Talking' by Harry Nilsson and 'Holding Back the Tears' by Simply Red. (This ii-V preogression never resolves to the I chord).

MODERN DANCE MUSIC

Modern programmers don't often look to music-theory rules for their chord sequences and may pick chords seemingly out of thin air for their unique sound. Sometimes a synth sound is programmed as a triad, enabling a keyboardist to sound a chord by hitting one key. Creating a single-line pattern with such a sound will result in a series of chords not necessarily in the major-scale chord sequence of the song.

For example, this is the effect one hears in the classic dance track by 2 Unlimited 'Get Ready for This', with the sequence (all major chords in key of E):

1 E-E-E

2 A-A-B-B

3 E-E-E

4 G-G-A-B

Hot Tip

A synthesizer can be programmed so that one key can produce three or more tones, enabling 'chord lines' that otherwise would be difficult to play.

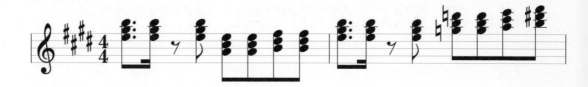

Above: Synth line based on major triad construction.

Accounting for Key

Although all the examples of note patterns and chords in this book are illustrated in the key of C, it's important to remember that they apply in any key. Though you may find it convenient to program a new song in the key of C (or its scale equivalent, Am) to utilize white notes on a keyboard, the rules about intervals and chords apply the same way in any key.

Thanks to modern computers, it's easy enough to transpose a key, say for a singer who needs the tune in a more comfortable range, with a few keystrokes. However, bear in mind that if you want to understand the tune in terms of music theory, a new key will mean different notes in the 'standard' scale of the new key.

GETTING MUSICAL WITH IT

Let's look at some other terms that we commonly use in making music. They can mean something entirely different to the music theorist than to the contemporary composer.

MELODY

The popular perception of a song's melody is a bit different in music theory. A melody (also tune, voice or line) is a linear succession of musical tones that the listener perceives as a single entity. It may be considered the foreground to the background accompaniment.

Some melodies may flow smoothly towards a dramatic peak, while others require acrobatic leaps to execute. Some melodies are little more than rhythmic stabs, while others are sweeping journeys of musical exploration.

Silent Night

Above: One of the most famous melodies in Western music, the hymn 'Silent Night'.

ARRANGEMENT

In music, an arrangement is a musical reworking of a previously composed work. It may differ from the original work by means of reharmonizing, orchestration or development of the formal structure.

Hot Tip

Melodies often consist of one or more musical phrases or motifs, and are usually repeated throughout a composition.

Arranging differs from orchestration. Orchestration is limited to the assignment of notes to instruments for performance by an orchestra or other musical ensemble. Arranging is creating something new from something that already exists.

Hungarian Dance No. 5

Above: A piece written on piano here arranged for five violins.

COUNTERPOINT

When you hear a line in a song that goes in a different direction or rhythm to the main line, you are hearing a counterpoint. An example would be guitar fills that shadow the vocal line, playing different melodies on top of or around the vocal.

Counterpoint In Popular Music

- In a country song, you might hear a steel guitar interacting with a banjo in counterpoint, as opposed to twin fiddles in the same song playing parallel harmony.

- The Beatles made more or less classical use of vocal counterpoint in songs like 'She's Leaving Home' and 'I've Got a Feeling'.

SEQUENCE

In your computer, a sequence is a data stream generated by a DAW (*see page 112*) but in music theory, a sequence is the immediate restatement of a melodic passage at a higher or lower pitch in the same voice. This kind of sequence has:

- Two segments, usually no more than three or four.

- Usually only one direction, continuingly higher or lower.

- Segments continuing by the same interval distance.

- The possibility for melody or harmony to form a sequence without the other participating.

Examples of Sequences

A well-known popular example of a threefold descending diatonic sequence is found in the refrain from the Christmas carol 'Angels We Have Heard on High', on the words "Glo ... ria in excelsis Deo". The one-bar melodic motive is shifted downward at the interval of a second, and the harmony moves in the same way.

A threefold sequence that ascends is the opening melody of Fats Waller's 'Ain't Misbehavin'.

Above: A descending sequence from 'Angels We Have Heard On High'.

SONIC RANGES

Any successful producer has to pay attention to the ranges of tones chosen for his or her instruments, lead voices and accompanying support sounds. Let's look at some concepts as they are defined in music theory.

DOWN LOW: BASS

Bass describes musical instruments that produce tones in the low-pitched range. Since producing low pitches usually requires a long air column or string, the string and wind bass instruments are usually the largest instruments in their families or instrument classes.

In electronic music, rap or drum and bass, bass notes are frequently used to provide a counterpoint or

Right: The bass is the largest instrument in the guitar family and has the lowest pitched range.

counter-melody. In popular
music the bass part most
often provides support,
playing the root or fifth of
the chord and stressing the
strong beats.

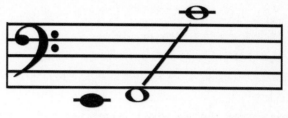

Above: Bass voice range on bass clef.

BASS VOICE

A bass is a type of classical male singing voice and has the lowest vocal range of all voice
types. A bass is typically classified as having a vocal range extending from around the second E
below middle C to the E above middle C, as shown in diagrams above and below.

BASS IN ARRANGEMENT

In computer music it's relatively easy to make the bass 'lock in' with programmed drums –
something that takes live bass players and drummers years to master. The combination of
good timing and complementary emphasis between the best drummers and bassists creates a
groove that is known as being 'in the pocket'.

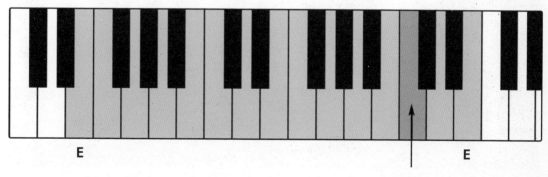

E   E

middle C

Above: Bass voice range on keyboard.

MID-RANGE SOUNDS

There is an accepted pattern in building a modern dance or pop arrangement. Typically, the drums are programmed first. The beat may come from something like a click track that establishes tempo for the other musicians or programmer.

Above: Many instruments compete for our ears' attention in the midrange of the frequency spectrum.

Getting The Mix Right

When it's time to add in keyboard and other mid-range parts, great care must be taken because these are the areas most likely to create a clashing or muddy mix. This is because the lead instrument, usually vocals, occupies a space right in the middle of our hearing range, and we want to focus on that lead sound.

Many instruments occupy the mid-range space and can interfere with our focus on the vocal. Some of these include:

- **Guitars**: A strumming acoustic guitar makes a great accompaniment to a vocal, but a distorted mid-range guitar can easily clash with or overpower a voice.

- **Horns**: Most effective for fills and accent parts, but potentially harmful to a mix when played over vocals. Tenor and alto saxophones often substitute for voices in solos and can compete negatively with them.

- **Strings**: Though typically sustained throughout a section and good for accompaniment, aggressive string parts should be used as fills or in their own break to avoid clashing with vocals.

- **Percussion**: Can help the groove along but can also distract from the lead instrument. The cowbell has become notorious for overpowering a mix.

Mid-range instruments, then, are essential to an effective arrangement but also potentially hazardous to it. Although a bass line can be too busy, out of time and out of tune, it doesn't have the same potential to clash negatively with a vocal, lead guitar or lead synth line.

HIGHER-PITCHED SOUNDS

As with mid-range sounds, it pays to be careful with tonalities at the higher end of the frequency range. Although not as likely to clash with lead instruments in the prime mid-range areas of vocals, guitars and saxes, higher-pitched instruments can become a distraction.

Some instruments to keep under control include:

- **High-frequency percussion**: Sounds like claves, shakers and synthesized percussion sounds can obliterate a carefully balanced mix.

- **Synth buzz**: A sound with wide filter sweeps can sound great by itself but wreak havoc in a mix. Always consider whether it conflicts with or distracts from a more important tonality.

- **Any strident or harsh sounds**: Even amazing technical feats of vocal gymnastics can become annoying if overused. Make sure the effect makes the impact desired and no more.

Though there are fewer rules about arranging from a music-theory standpoint compared with classical writing or orchestral arranging, the computer musician still has to be judicious about the sonic and musical balance of all parts, just as the eighteenth-century symphonic composer or arranger had to.

WORKING IN THE BOX

NOTES IN THE COMPUTER

Although computers can never entirely replace humans in the composing and arranging of music, the machines have brought an exciting level of precision to performance. Now, electronic music performance can be as humanly expressive – or robotically monotonous – as desired.

THE DIGITAL AUDIO WORKSTATION

The most important piece of software in music making is the digital audio workstation (or DAW). These programs (other than Avid Pro Tools) started out as MIDI sequencers – recording and

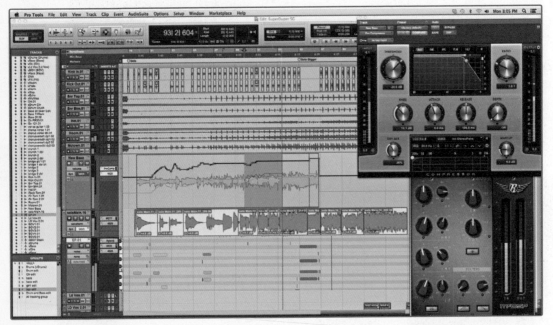

Above: Digital Audio Workstations (DAWs), like Pro Tools, excel at placing musical events at very precise points in time.

playing back streams of MIDI data to a synthesizer or drum machine, in the same way a piano roll enabled playback on a player piano a hundred years before.

Eventually, these programs added audio recording capability to their MIDI abilities, including the ability to speak the language of traditional music theory as well as the language of bits and bytes. This was possible because computers excel at reproducing musical events at specific spots in time.

SPACE AND TIME

Every DAW can create a sequence of data (it may be called a song, a project, a sequence or something else) that has multiple ways to divide the data into manageable groups. A songwriter or traditional composer can decide to section his or her project into bars and beats as on manuscript paper, while a film scorer or Foley effects person may only need a continuous time reference (hours, minutes, seconds) for a project.

What gives such detailed control on a computer is that a computer can use a much higher resolution (see below) than that which can be indicated on a piece of manuscript paper. A composer can indicate in a few ways on paper how he or she would like a player to perform the piece in time, but a computer can execute that piece with almost infinite precision.

RESOLUTION

A DAW like Apple's Logic Pro X can utilize a resolution of 960 pulses per crotchet (PPQ), also known as ticks. This means that, in a 4/4 bar of music, there are 3,840 possible places for a note to fall. The faster the tempo, the closer together those slots are, meaning a producer or programmer has almost no limits on the placement of notes. Even at slower tempos, 960 ticks is more resolution than most composers need.

Hot Tip

Computers can generate impeccable timing but they can also sound robotic and monotonous.

PLACING NOTES

In a computer, musical notes are entered via a MIDI keyboard or percussion pads. For those who don't read music, graphic representations were devised that depict a musical note as a horizontal bar on a grid where the x-axis equals time and the y-axis equals pitch. The length of the graphic bar indicates its duration.

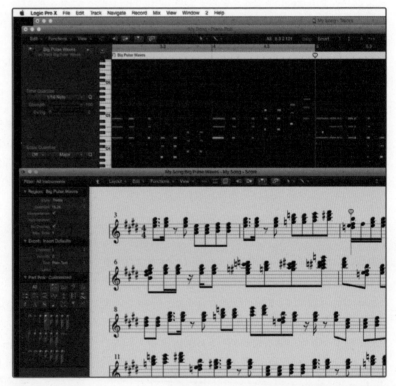

Left: The extensive score editing tools in Logic Pro X.

Above: Notes in a score window and the corresponding representation in a MIDI 'piano roll' window.

SCORE EDITING FEATURES

Modern DAW software gives great advantage to your pursuit of music-theory knowledge by updating its score window as you make changes to your MIDI tracks.

In a score editor, you can enter markings directly using a specified tools palette, such as the one in Logic Pro X, which provides tools for direct entry of notes, rests, dynamic markings and a multitude of other music symbols on your project score.

> **Hot Tip**
>
> **The graphic representation of notes in a DAW is often called a 'piano roll' editor because of its resemblance to the punched paper rolls that used to drive a player piano.**

As good as the score editor of a DAW may be, it might come up short when compared to the capabilities of dedicated music engraving programs (*see right*), which are capable of importing a composition by MIDI and transcribing the file's musical data to a highly detailed written score.

Right: Dedicated music engraving programs like Finale have an extensive tool set for creating and exporting printed music.

EXPANDING YOUR HORIZONS

By now it should be clear that we have only scratched the surface of music theory. Serious composers have been grounded in these rules for centuries, and a full understanding only comes with serious study over years or a lifetime of studying other composers and their techniques.

TURNING THEORY INTO PRACTICE

But as a modern computer musician you may need only a fraction of this knowledge to make a big impact on your own songs and productions. For example, knowing which chords work in which keys is crucial to every type of music from smooth jazz to acid rock.

So how do you take this basic exposure to music theory and apply it to your own work? To start with, analyse as many other songs and recordings as you can.

LISTEN, LISTEN, LISTEN

The best way to understand music is to listen to and deconstruct as much of it as you can. Generations of twentieth-century music fans grew up playing sections of a vinyl recording or tape over and over again as they tried to duplicate inspiring sections on their own guitars, pianos or voices.

Today, there are easier ways to analyse common musical passages and compare what you hear to the theoretical knowledge you've picked up. Here are some useful products that can help you.

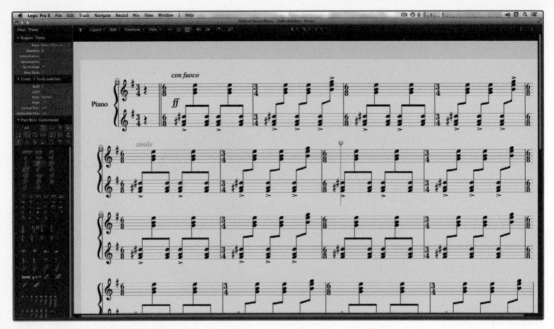

Above: Logic Pro X score editor.

DIGITAL AUDIO WORKSTATION SOFTWARE

Since you are a computer musician, you may already have one of these. Here are some of the most popular ones.

Apple Logic Pro X

Logic Pro X, like all major DAW software, lets you view your MIDI tracks in musical notation. Logic Pro X also comes with an extensive library of sounds to help you get going quickly with your compositions.

Avid Pro Tools

The granddaddy of pro DAW software, Pro Tools added MIDI functionality and a score editor later than other DAWs that began as MIDI sequencers.

Above: Pro Tools score editor.

However, its capabilities now rival those of its competitors.

Digital Performer

Digital Performer is another pro-level DAW with extensive MIDI capability. It can import and convert MIDI files into standard

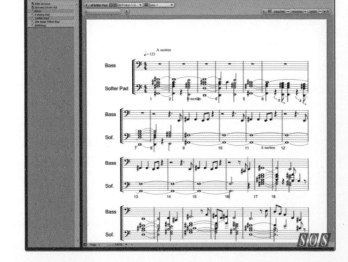

Right: Digital Performer's QuickScribe score editor.

Above: Cubase score editor.

Cubase

Cubase began as a MIDI sequencer before inventing the VST plug-in format. Its newer versions have extensive notation editing features.

DEDICATED SCORE EDITING SOFTWARE

In addition to the notation capabilities of DAW software, there are dedicated programs designed from the ground up for printing musical scores. With a full complement of tools for making every kind of standard and advanced mark-up, these programs are in the elite class of music document preparation.

MakeMusic Finale

Finale is the flagship program of a series of proprietary scorewriters created by MakeMusic for PCs and Macs. MakeMusic also offers less expensive versions of Finale, with subsets of the

Above: MakeMusic's Finale allows you to arrange or compose publisher-quality scores that play back.

main program's features. These include SongWriter and PrintMusic, as well as a freeware program, Finale Notepad, which allows only rudimentary editing.

Sibelius

Sibelius is a scorewriter program used by composers, arrangers, performers, music publishers, teachers and students,

Hot Tip

Modern DAWs let you edit cut, copy and add notes directly into musical notation. If you change a note value, the software automatically updates flags, beams and rests.

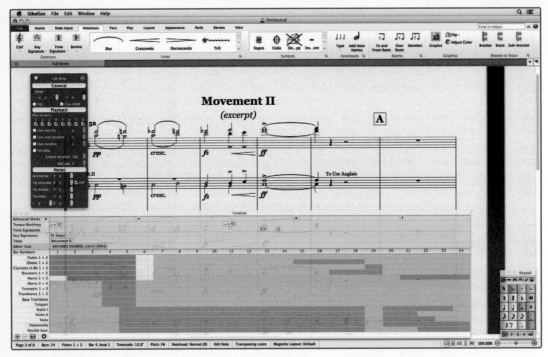

Above: Sibelius enables the user to create, print and play back sheet music, and publish it via the internet or iPad.

particularly for writing classical, jazz, band, vocal, film and television music. In addition to editing and printing scores, Sibelius can also play music back using synthesized sounds, produce legible scores for editing and printing, and publish scores for others to access via the internet and iPad.

AudioScore Ultimate

Sibelius also markets AudioScore Ultimate, which lets you open a CD track or MP3 file and transcribe it to a score. The software employs technology to convert up to 16 instruments or

Hot Tip

Music engraving programs like Finale and Sibelius let you create music notation as complex as your imagination requires.

notes at a time into multiple staves, with up to four voices per stave.

PreSonus Notion

Notion is a program for music composition and performance for Windows and Mac OS. Notion's sample library for playback was recorded at Abbey Road by the London Symphony Orchestra. Notion Music also offers other programs such as Protege (similar to Notion with limited functionality), Progression (a composition program oriented to guitarists) and Notion Conducting (for conducting classes).

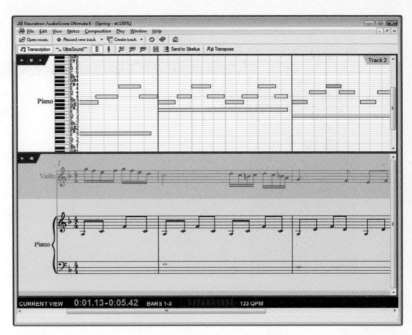

Above: As well as allowing you to transcribe scores from CDs and MP3s, AudioScore Ultimate enables you to print a professional-quality score.

Right: PreSonus Notion enables you to compose and edit music, then hear it played back using the software's world-class sample library.

Above: A pre-arranged MIDI file loaded into Logic Pro X.

MIDI FILE IMPORT

One way to learn about music on the written page is to import pre-arranged MIDI files into your DAW and view them in its score editor. You can generate a written score of all parts.

EDITING WINDOWS

The integration of score editors within major DAWs is sophisticated and seamless. Dragging a note's duration from, say, a quantized 120 ticks to 240 ticks will simultaneously change the corresponding note in the score editor from a semiquaver to a quaver.

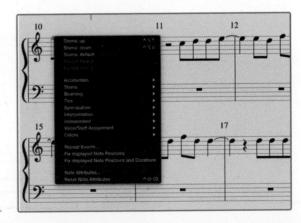

Right: A pre-arranged MIDI file loaded into Logic Pro X.

Alternatively, right-clicking on a note in the score editor will bring up a contextual menu of options for editing notes if you prefer to edit in the score window. Although each DAW has different conventions and commands, all provide this editing capability.

FROM THE DIGITAL TO THE THEORETICAL

Music theory is not an absolute requirement for making great music on a computer, or with an instrument for that matter. But if you want a thorough understanding of these ideas and processes you may want to further explore the concepts presented in this book by examining the references and websites on the following page.

USEFUL WEBSITES AND FURTHER READING

WEBSITES

www.donrathjr.com
An extensive music-related site with reviews as well as lessons.

www.essential-music-theory.com
Introductory lessons tied to a book.

www.method-behind-the-music.com
A simple but thorough examination of theoretical concepts.

www.musictheoryblog.blogspot.com
Extensive lessons.

www.mymusictheory.com
A site with all the basics divided by grade.

www.openmusictheory.com
An open-source textbook-style collection of lessons.

www.tobyrush.com/theorypages/index
The fundamentals of music theory in an engaging comic-style format.

www.youtube.com/playlist?list=PLC720D5DC4468B9B1
A collection of videos in a series titled 'How Music Works'.

FURTHER READING

Harnum, Jonathan, *Basic Music Theory*, Sol-Ut Press, 2001.

Jones, George Thaddeus, *Music Theory*, Harper Perennial, 1974.

Laitz, Steven G., *The Complete Musician*, 2008.

Miller, Michael, *The Complete Idiot's Guide to Music Theory*, Alpha, 2005.

Pilhofer, Michael and Day, Holly, *Music Theory for Dummies*, Wiley, 2007.

Sorce, Richard, *Music Theory for the Music Professional*, Ardsley House, 1995.

Taylor, Eric, *First Steps in Music Theory*, ABRSM, 1999.

Willmott, Bret, *Complete Book of Harmony, Theory and Voicing*, Mel Bay, 1994.

INDEX